Wood of Plane

Poems

Domenico Corna

ISBN: 9791281450097

Website: www.domenicocorna.it
e-mail: domenico@domenicocorna.it

The intuition of a poet belongs to everyone because that intuition comes from everyone. I present things I don't know, which come from another part of me. Sometimes I understand the meaning; sometimes I don't. I feel pain and joy—the source of which is unknown—that touch me softly or strongly, changing my vision of life.

Domenico Corna

Index

We started walking together, followers of fantasy, without running. Timeless memories, hidden in the dark, are strange thoughts that lead us. We keep one dream alive, hand in hand, while our souls overlap, until the end of the path.

1. We Started

Our path begins with the need to free ourselves from the weight of our social importance, abandoning privilege's ambition and success. In the twilight, without certainty, between fear and loneliness, the confidence from our dreams will accompany us. We will measure our determination to continue to go on beyond logic.

Our Dream

Our dream today is like the sun,
like its tears of rain
over our cloud of tissue paper.

Closing our eyes, the flight began
around the curved lines of the paths,
under the rain, the sun and among endless woods.

The great heights and precipices
are a thousand thoughts, colors and scents
who will not abandon us upon their return.

On this journey towards the sun,
on our cloud of tissue paper,
a key and a hope accompany us.

You are hope, and I have the key,
even if the wait is likely to dissolve
the perseverance of any desire.

The Madness

Tell me the face of those who saw you cry.
Tell me the words never said
while laughing at your dreams of freedom and distant
destinations.

Tell me about their arrogant commiseration,
the hypocrisy of that false and useless love
to get you away from a madness for you so seductive.

No, you weren't talking about revolution
when you decided to stop looking for a reason
and started following those unknown limits.

You found the darkness lying on immense prairies,
unimaginable mountains illuminated by your dreams,
then the rain, so much sun and the desire not to
return.

With your eyes closed to the unknown,
you rode a mysterious wind
between fear, tears of pain
and the instinct to never come back.

Tell me what you think now of our life
while you fly free to be where and when you want,
over the thousand meadows and flowers of your
universe.

Tell me what you think now of all of us—
many small insects unnecessarily busy researching
a role and a thousand stupid satisfactions?

A New Shoot

In a far corner,
in this, my old youth,
soaked by stupid memories,
from an old, dry branch,
a new shoot has awakened
and asks to play with the sun.

How will I behave with a new bud
of his thousand loves' desires,
in my spirit inclined to slowness
and the wisdom of the sunset?

She wants me to abandon my loneliness,
to resume playing,
challenging the headwind
to the next solitary thousand destinations.

Who? Are you talking about me?
An old horse with his ears down
and the gaze always fixed up there
waiting for my moon?

She has given me this sweet surprise
and laughs among a thousand thunders and lightning.
"Don't worry! You'll come to the beginning," she
whispers.
"But now a new sun is waiting for you.
Run! Soon it's springtime."

Manolo

I had a sad thought about you.
I felt it this morning
when they told me.
Thinking of you no more present,
in the most incomprehensible of choices,
gave me a sense of fright.

Good night to you.
On your difficult journey
in search of light
you'll go through every darkness,
suffering, stumbling,
looking for an unstable certainty.

Good trip, my friend—
so lost and distant
from the radiant days.
I know one day I'll see you again.
You will bring me the safe route as a gift
to win my darkness, too.

Alone

This night,
even the sparks
swinging on the chandelier,
soft as meteorites,
don't want to keep me company.

They prefer to dissolve away
around other lights,
other cries or any laments
but full of feeling.

Yet it was only yesterday
when, on my face, tired
from lament and loneliness,
the smile was back.

Today I am alone
in this room full of remorse
and useless expedients.
No one else meets my hand.
No one else meets my sadness.

Sweet Break

Get a blue sky and paint it red
in this night, deep like a dream,
in this need to have and to give.

Autumn is spring from my window,
in an ancient romantic dream,
in this desire to become.

If I close my eyes, I can have you here,
on a long, lonely road
and a sweet song is taking us away.

It's an endless journey to the horizon
in the colors of the rainbow,
beyond the limits of imagination.

I don't want to wake up from this long dream,
back to a dawn without any fantasy,
among its sad, dark inhabitants.

But among gray solitudes,
a colorful smile walks with my normality,
waiting to fly back to the sky.

Distant Prairies

"You will go far away,
rhythmically swaying,
just as before, against the wind
while you learn to love
even if you are suffering.

"At last, the time will come
of distant prairies,
of buffaloes under the sun,
of deep silence and shining moons
to be touched with your fingers.

"You will fly toward the sun—
through the eye of a storm—
in the contours of the pink hills
resting on the desert
like an old man on the balcony."

Where am I going now
if the moon is just a light,
and when it rains nothing else goes down
except drops of tears
and sighs of sadness?

"I know! It's only a dream.
From that window,
the world is still the same.
But sometimes, if you're silent,
you can feel their distant fragrance."

My Path

Born from the past and the wind,
I rode an old storm
to see the clouds flowing upside down—
one for every year of loneliness.

I have opened the book of my life
with its images carved to relief,
with its unknown flavors
coming from the other part of me.

Time, misfortune and miracles had dissolved them—
one for each drop of rain,
leaving me the wonder
about the strange instinct to keep them together.

I'm here. I'm the storm.
For every drop that falls, I lose a cloud.
I turned myself into rain, wind and sun
to rebuild my life.

Good Night

Good night to your world of dreams.
It will never be dark behind your eyes;
another sun, another voice
will guide you on your path.

Good night to your open hands.
The night will disperse your fears;
it will hang on the stars and the moon
like clothes hung to dry.

Good night to your smile
meeting at the fairest of the sunsets,
where countless colored crayons
are mapping the horizon.

Good night to your smooth breathing—
to your soul full of life.
To the day that has entrusted it,
the night will return it more beautiful.

11

12

2. Walking Together

No one is ever alone while walking alone. Sometimes, reading the same expression on the face of someone who passes by, we discover how others are walking the same path as us. Everyone, alone, walks together, holding hands.

We All

Certainly, I'll be happy
when I come to you,
bringing myself
in my songs.

How nice it will be
greet each other without talking
and run around the world
just looking into each other's eyes.

Oh, yes! We'll find love again—
we defeated, outcast…
we will grow flowers.

We will join
our childhoods—all the same,
our fears like the clouds of a thunderstorm.

We will rain with joy,
our hearts, like a river,
running down to the sea.

Oh, yes! We'll find love again—
we who have been defeated, outcast…
we will grow flowers.

Molly Little Small Cloud

Molly—a little, small cloud
sails the blue sky
with her snowflakes
to meet her fate.

A little small cloud
flowing through my desires
has come straight
to my heart.

If I couldn't fly,
what would my life be?
If I couldn't change my destiny,
what would freedom taste like?

I want a little love, too,
a little warmth in my heart—
as a gift looking for a smile
from a child's yelp of joy.

Little small cloud in the blue sky,
holding your flakes close,
give me your hand.
Maybe we will travel together.

The Ancient Train

Maybe in pain,
between loneliness
and unawareness,
naked and staring,

we shall sit—
immersed in memories,
slow and deformable
and nothing more—

on an ancient train
driven by fate,
between intuitions
and reflected images.

Maybe the wind
beyond the horizon,
beyond this world,
will dissolve us,

or God himself
will comfort our weeping,
turning into certainty
the ancient faith

or just one moment.
But the unhappiness will be filled
on that train
to a new beginning.

Can You Hear Me?

Can you hear me
even if the tiredness of the path
carries away all the promises?
Even if, from the glass of your window,
the sky is blocked like an old, broken car
and the fear, turning into a storm,
shocked up with its impetuosity
all the times we met,
all the times we put off until tomorrow
the wish to be understood?

Please remember…
on another morning,
thoughts were running free,
and the sky was beyond the picture on the wall.
We were endlessly bounding, holding hands,
beyond all the thunderstorms,
over all the colors of the rainbow.
Looking into your eyes, I said,
"Will you be able to hear me
even when the lights are switched off
and just a faint whisper can reach you?"

Imperfect Waves

The sea behind the mountain
shows itself
as uncultivated fields
of nostalgia
in a long stretch of solitude,
poor but full of light.
Flowers grow among the waves
and creep slowly,
discovering always fresh sprouts
and shining moons to make them grow.
And then the ships—
slow, dark-dressed ladies—
obscure the reflections of the sun,
and force it to slip
right on the beach,
where the sand plays
with the waves—
their soft mouths and smiles.
Then the sea disperses them as thoughts,
as the children at sunset,
resuming the backwash by the hand,
taking away even the imperfect waves.

We Are Alone

No need for a phone ringing
or a sunny day
after so much rain.

In this room,
books and music
drip only sadness.

Out in the street, people are laughing.
They fly like swallows
from tree to tree.

Instead, she has taken my wings.
Here, sitting beside me,
she will not let me go.

We are alone in our night.
Of the sun passing by,
we distinguish only its shadows.

Without Honor and Glory

I love your smile,
the gift of you so disinterested
to make you great,
your loneliness,
your good intentions,
and sighs steeped in sadness.

Your prayers
are dialogue and meditation.
You talk with the wind
as if it were God,
inciting him closely
to share your life.

You want joy and pain
to accompany you
while you are making love
like two newlyweds,
far away from fast cars
and impertinent highways.

You hold hands
in a slow walk
on a country road,
little more than alone,
fascinated by this life
without honor and glory.

Wild Horses

Wild horses
toward the sun;
tonight, they will sleep among the stars,
embracing each other like young colts.

I know there are problems down here;
the wind brings only sad news,
and our hearts seem like sheets of ice
every time we look into the eyes
of those who pass us by.

But we know how to wait,
when the most generous sun
will make the snowdrops grow,
melting beneath it
a huge prairie.

We'll be all together,
ready to follow our desires
and take off
like wild horses
en route to the stars.

Who Knows If You Still Believe?

Who knows if you still believe
if you wake up in the morning
happy to start living
a new day?

If rain and insults
have stolen your smile
and the anger has contorted
your poor heart?

If you go to work
full of thoughts of battle,
looking like
a beleaguered captain?

Who knows if, in the morning,
coming out of the front door,
you look again to the daisies
newly blossomed in the meadow?

If you greet again with a smile
the blackbird who lives on your roof—
the one who eats the strawberries—
you have planted with so much love?

Domenico Corna

3. Followers of Fantasy

Hidden personalities are within us that only the imagination can bring out. They arise, producing moments of elation, depression, and irrational tears. We learn to hide the heat in our hearts, as well as the sadness. Nobody realizes our happiness or our tears hidden behind two smiling eyes.

Stones and Shells

Not only between mountains and beaches
are born stones and shells,
like true fruits of a season.

Here, too, the sea flows into the closet,
and glaciers spill out from the drawers
between patches and mothballs.

There are uncommon places,
in which life and death shake hands
to share pleasure and pain,

where the silence marks a life—
dressed by stones, shells,
oceans and endless prairies.

Between the Sun, Moon, and Stars

Now close your eyes,
and try again
to get lost in the green meadows
just touching the blades of grass.

A violin is in your desires
to color the music
so, the trip will be soft
among the sun, moon, and stars.

The voice nuanced in a rainbow
is now, today, yesterday,
many years ago, always
remembering the first Eden.

If you have started looking,
free the insights
forced by pain
to where they will carry you.

It will only take a moment
before your eyes open,
but without pain,
between the sun, moon, and stars.

Montisola Evenings

Thin and soft,
Montisola evenings
rain down on us.

The fireflies, thoughts,
the soft sensations
meet at sunset.

It releases the desire
between the sky and the lake
and touches the mountain.

The forest nearby
is full of omens:
gnomes and owls in the night,

dragons, fairies, and witches
performing their rituals,
silver and black coloring.

Time has denied us,
away, far beyond that lake
among other lights, other omens.

We contemplate the insights,
followers of the imagination.
On the other side, you are running.

I See the Life

I see the life—
shyness dressed,
enclosed like a flower.

Your fragrance
came with the wind
that brought you here.

You have enlightened somebody
after you were freed
from the arms of love.

You have taken him in your hands
while blooming
in the beauty.

Now you come here,
entangled
in a poem.

To Budapest

The road ran between my thoughts
before my car became silent,
welcoming metamorphosing music.

Now colored confetti fall slowly,
leaning on a rainbow-colored expanse,
cars like coffee pots steaming sway to the guitar
rhythm.

The great happy river is playing the piano
while sipping its cotton candy trees;
sad and meek reindeer are looking for their Santa
Claus.

Uninhibited ladies with big, colorful hats
in a slow dance tempt me with their fruits.
I look at them and run away, blushing.

My car moves frantically its snout
following a solo guitar
dissolving like the smoke of the fire.

The great city is right there at the end;
I wonder if it will welcome me with a smile.
Will it accept my imagination as a gift?

Flying

I close my eyes and feel myself alone,
walking between dull sounds,
breathing the ancient stories
in the thrill of the night.

I look around into an abyss that scares me.
Everything is distant.
After gliding through a dark valley,
I will perch upon a bell tower.

I come back only late at night.
Please, let my bed be unmade
So, I don't realize
that another night is done.

I will come back staggering—
drunken by fantasy,
and I will leave that life.
Bring me back again to its melancholy.

Imagination

I am here dreamy
on an old chair
outside the door, next to the dark,
seduced by the thoughts,
by the best among the sunsets—
a sweet imperfection,
the last of the day, the more persuasive
fled from the harmony
that always protects those who live.

She stole my thoughts,
even the most solitary,
giving the impression of eternity.
With the world in the palm of my hand
and the moon on my shoulders,
I am looking among my wishes,
the same as always,
the most hidden and secret,
because they don't lose time anymore
to take me away.

If I Could

I don't have the gift of wings,
even though I often take flight.

But this joy, if I could,
I would keep squeezed between my fingers.

Instead, often my thinking
leaves emotions,

instead of dreaming in freedom
goes back to the usual practices.

Shiny Lake

One day, when I die, I will come to you.
I will ask the God of heaven
to turn me into water,
playing with your waves.

One day, when I die, I will come to you.
I will ask to stay close to you,
my ashes like snow,
with your wind and your butterflies.

One day, when I die, I will come to you—
leaving me silently
next to your depth,
to hear your voice.

One day, when I die, I will come to you—
drinking your beauty,
breathing your wisdom,
falling asleep into your night.

4. Without Running

After each small victory, we seem to be close to the goal. But we learn the value of patience in accepting that everything runs smoothly as planned. Lost opportunities and denied destinations deeply mark our spirit with the feeling of being persecuted by an unfavorable destiny.

Dawn of My Sunset

The rain had just ended
at the dawn of my sunset,
when the rainbow showed me
that invisible path.

No more trees to limit the horizon,
nor meadows awaiting the call of the dew,
but a smile as big as the horizon
and immense opportunities to play with.

I left my house without looking back,
and, after shaking off the last drops,
I saw your face become sad
for not being able to company me.

How I wish that darkness surprised you
with the magical colors of the seasons
without envy the birds chasing each other,
waiting for migration.

But be happy! They belong to you now;
you will aspire to all my dreams—
will mix tears and rain
like flowers in a thunderstorm.

I'll always be here in the Wood of Plane,
waiting like a spiteful bug,
this time to walk together,
making fun of life.

The Eyes of Tomorrow

If I had the eyes of tomorrow,
I would not load up memories
of this sunset in autumn.
I would not be fantasizing
about what life takes.
I would consider now
what stands before me
before it slips away.

If I had the eyes of tomorrow,
I would love this room—
its dim light,
its mystical perfume.
I would be carried away
by the voices from the street
because they guide my thoughts.
I would caress once again
Romeo sleeping in the basket.

If I had the eyes of tomorrow,
I would go down the stairs,
and, to your eyes in disbelief,
I would give this sun
before its sunset.
I would stop this moment
because it becomes eternal.

Moon and Us

The streetcar tracks and thoughts—
near home, I close my eyes
to the lights and sad sounds.

It's a traffic light always yellow.
That tree born from the cement
has reached my window.

Embracing, we dream of other colors,
other silences filled with snow
and dazzling springs.

Between us rises a bold moon,
climbing a skyscraper
with her half-sad smile.

She carries the song of crickets,
coming back from the mountains
from her path on the sea.

Inside her, we reflect
as we finally begin
to live away from here.

I'll Be There

Want to bet I'll be there
when, in need, you call me?
I'll be right there next to you.

Have no doubts about your choice;
don't look back in regret.
Go ahead across your path.

I love your voice when you don't say a word;
I can feel it in your thoughts,
which don't give me any other options.

I love your affection—
your endless imagination,
and your dreams that take me away.

Don't try to find me;
don't try to catch me because I'm already here,
between your thoughts and your dreams.

Without Getting Lost

The events that run
rebuild your image—
indefinable as the rain
that falls into a subtle sadness.

Cheeky angels have planned
your last flight, too
until you rise to the rainbow,
hiding yourself in the rain.

The water coming back to the sky
has darkened the horizon
in an event to be reconstructed,
in a ticket to get back.

Now time is playing
with the wish to conciliate
the fear with the pleasure
in the ritual of hope.

You'll be here,
without the fear of coming back,
within that sensation of pride
that makes you rise after every fall.

Next to an Owl

When the night comes,
I am not happy
if uncontrollable thoughts
hang the moon on the trees
and share my nostalgia.

Sometimes I prefer to cling
to the night guardian,
to a cloud of fireflies,
to support my fears
and make them comprehensible.

Here, next to an owl,
I breathe deeply,
looking around with his eyes.
Even the life passing by
cannot notice me.

Now our sooty smiles
run through the dark countryside
between the tops of the pines,
on its night wings,
and go far away.

The Old River

On the bank of the old river,
we look in amazement
at the old, dusty roads
patiently smoothed
by rain and sun
greeting its gentle flow.

The insights,
silence, and patience
mark
its adult age
and its destiny.

It has hugged in a mirror
a thousand loves and tears
on their way to the sea,
between lost grasses
and old broken branches.

It soothes their pain,
turning the echoes
of deep breaths
into soft swirls
that only fish can hear.

Unconsciously, we jump
into its waves,
among broken dreams
and love stories,
already holding hands.

That Day Will Come

The day will come of blue thoughts
born from the nightly hot sun,
from fervent imaginations
spread out by the wind like clusters in October
ready for harvesting.

Over there, the infinite are memories—
flowers open at dusk,
fed by ripe moons,
and sighs barely hinted at,
like children's dreams.

You will fall asleep on soft beaches.
You will keep the sun and the moon
attached to a balloon,
dancing happily
as if at a small-town party.

You will dream in her eyes,
bluer than your thoughts,
today as yesterday,
near and far,
lost in fantasy.

Two Old Shoes

Two old shoes
lying sadly
between gray dust and memories
in a forgotten corner
away from strong light.

Time does not care
about their memories—
about a heartfelt presence
hung on their story.

Life has slowly dissolved
as an ancient tale—
like children at sunset
and their mysterious thoughts.

The dreams of all the roads
and the many hidden lives
exist within a penumbra.
Here, the light is too strong
and cravings too impetuous.

Domenico Corna

5. Timeless Memories

Timeless memories haphazardly emerge, not only changing our vision of life but also revealing old emotions far away over time. Like flashes of light in the darkness, we must grasp them before they slip away, making sure they come back to be part of us. They will help us when the darkness comes.

Give Me a Memory

If you walk beside me,
here where I'm resting,
and if my image
back in your mind—
although too busy,
give me a memory.

Remember for me the scent of the fields
after a rainy day,
the sunrise, the sunset,
and the road that runs slowly
back home.

Stay here over me for a little while.
Touch me with your imagination.
Exchange these sad flowers
with the scent of freshly baked bread
and the taste of wine near fermentation.

I'll give you back the home fragrance,
the dreams that came true,
unhappiness and loneliness,
which eventually fill up
while time opens
the door of the infinite.

I will follow you up to your sunset.
I'll chase away the fear of your night.
We will be together—a memory—a smile.

A Little Tied Affection

If sometimes I guess you're not here
waking me up in the morning.
If sometimes I see happiness in the other's look
and think it has been stolen.

It's the pain that keeps me close,
and imagination does not help me anymore.

You wanted to be part
of clear evenings,
of sound barely hinted
that preludes the melody,
of softer colors
of sunrise and sunset.

Now your thought has become free
and runs without limitation.
I wonder if you still remember
a little tied affection.

When I Close My Eyes

Sometimes I meet happy thoughts in the night
that urge the memory
like old flashes of a storm,
like the dim light of a candle
swinging slowly,
drunk in the night.

Maybe someone, hidden in the shadows,
is calling,
inviting me,
with little thoughts,
to close my eyelids
and let go.

It's an incomprehensible trip,
where space does not exist,
where the dim light of the evening
becomes an impression of eternity,
hand in hand with a smile
that cannot be only imaginary.

The Stairs

I climb the stairs to come back,
the ones softened by time,
mollified by the rain.
I gather, looking around.

On a yellowed table,
now the flowers bloom,
dissolving the indifference
into cotton candy.

The dusty road
that brought us here yesterday
surely has not gone away.
It's waiting as you wanted.

But today I can see a new world
just started from here,
between branches always twisted
and a pungent smell of mold.

In front of the door, I linger—
how would it have been without you?
Inside, in the middle of the light,
I wonder if you're thinking of me.

Music

If it will come,
dense and full of mystery,
in this afternoon,
here, between flowering plants, ditches,
and waving grasses, into the water,
between fields flooded by the sun,

if it will play
with flies, sleepy with nostalgia,
the only ones waiting for an unseemly gesture
to go back to flying,

just this night,
the sky will not change his blue
even sarcastic and overbearing.

It will find
the dark night's flowers flourish,
the ones only the moon can make shine.

Maybe tonight there will be music.
Sometimes the violins sing;
sometimes they speak.

Song of Nostalgia

The sunlight slowly slips between the stones,
coloring the dark hidden inside their crevices,

flowing the contours of the slow clouds
immersed in the lake, in its deep nostalgia.

Far, far away—lost.
The memory is confused,
turns on itself,
does not want to play anymore.

The first rays of the dark walk fast,
chasing the sun, taking back its stones.

Helplessly, I'm surprised by one cloud far away;
it hides the sun and steals my fantasy.

My thoughts fly far away, leaving me alone
on the sunset's edge, on the border's life.

So, I sail slowly—lost in melancholy,
inside a dream too young to be courted.

Other Shores

If, in the morning, you go away before I awake
to escape the pain of the memories,
and you leave me here counting your dreams,
I will accept I will caress you no more.

If, in the evening, you look for a reason to forget me,
in solitude, away from your memories,
forgetting the red clouds on the horizon,
I will accept I will not be the one to guide your eyes.

But something can happen
if, deep in your thoughts,
a bit of nostalgia brings your thought back to me;
we'll be closer than we've ever been.

Sometime at Night

When I look at the world
sitting beside my dreams
on these nights when everything seems to shine,
and the fog covers the Earth
as a loving mother,
I think of harmony,
I think of love,
of everything that was stolen from us,
offering in return a destiny
wrapped in a sad cloak.

There were other long nights
when we were together,
counting the stars one by one,
and you were talking to me.
"I want to stay beside you
because my heart can't resist.
I think of harmony,
I think of love,
of everything that was stolen from us.
I can't shine
if you're not here with me."

The Sunset

If, after daytime,
when the sun goes down,
you grab the sunny breath,
and your eyes don't see
only tired horizons
but many changing seasons
and multicolored skies
with soft and fluffy clouds,

in your heart there will be something
more precious than every breath.
It will take you far away,
even if, in the morning,
your drowsy mind
refuses to believe,
and your heart is so tired
that it's no longer able to dream.

6. Hidden in the Dark

When darkness falls and we discover that there is no place where we can escape and that there is no positive thinking to be superimposed to decrease its strength, timeless memories bring the flavor of ancient battles in accepting those fears. We will take the strength from our weakness to meet our darkness without running away.

Unusual Ray

It could have been a confused image
fled from its restricted access,
the one wandering the city sidewalks,
amid the black and purple shadows
born from park benches,
from the background pain of a siren,
cats, cars, and figures sniffing each other.

It was born while the sun was going down,
such as the perennial memory
that will not shatter.
We thought it was a sign,
a kind of premonition,
a god who, abandoning the others' pain,
was also thinking a little about us.

Instead, it was the reflection of a smile—
one last warm ray of sunshine
that, stubborn in the evening,
still was lighting the town,
mirroring itself
from the window of a skyscraper.

Downstairs

Don't be afraid to walk downstairs,
to discover the darkness of your soul.
With every step, the light fades,
black impressions in your mind;
your eyes can't answer
the need to be somewhere else.

Down, down, deeper and deeper,
you'll meet you and your soul—
ineffable, sweet, magical fear,
end of life, a promontory of the infinite,
wonderful game of rebirth.

Your fears will disappear,
discovering another light in the dark,
the same one lighting a thousand other worlds
where you've been and will go back to.

You will want to stay forever—
spectator and magic protagonist,
but, meeting my hand,
I'll free you from your immensity
making you climb the stairs in reverse.
You will be ready to restart,
but this time together.

Looking at Your Eyes

When I look into your eyes, I am confused.
Where were you when my heart was bursting?
When fear stole my desire to live
and the night was so close inside of me?

I see your quiet face far away—
too far away.
Where were you when evil took possession of me,
when the thought stopped dreaming?

Pain calls me again.
If you're not here, there is no hope.
Leave your sweet dreams and run to me,
but do it before the night takes me away.

When I look into your eyes, I am confused.
You're here, but I don't know if you understand.
I love your hand caressing me again.
How many times I've dreamed of your smile.

Please, let's run away—you and I.
I'll be silent without bothering you.
I'll hold you only when the night comes,
dreaming once again to be in you.

Only the Silence

Under the irreverent light
of this street lamp,
life is illuminated.

With sliding tires,
a car is wrecked
with its shining eyes.

An old, disused hero
dangles—uncertain and breathless—
forsaken as a toy,

then turns the corner,
clinging to the wall
like a bas-relief.

With his wise nose,
a stray dog
is looking for a reason.

And beyond, nothing more—
only silence remains,
blacker than the night.

A Confused Message

I will not follow
a confused message
coming from afar
that leads me
to search for
unfertile satisfactions.

I will wait
in the cornfields
higher than my head,
the skinned knees
and sewn rags
forming flags.

Behind a window,
disguised as a dream,
someone waits for me
to lull my lonely nights
with smiles, tears,
and tender hugging.

I pray
that the sunset
and its shadows
come soon.
Somebody waits
to warm my night.

A Clear Message

I never imagined
I would follow a smile
and a strange finger
pointing in one direction,
saying, "Go ahead!
Collect your dreams
like fresh fruits of the season."

Now I see
long roads to travel
and many others to imagine.

She promised me two lives:
one to live
and another to invent,
a gift far away
from all the interpretation
opened to every choice.

The gift is the fantasy,
a figment of the imagination,
that brings me closer to her.

I Saw You in the Trench

I saw you in the trench,
fighting with your thoughts
while outside the war raged—
that strange epidemic involving everyone.
Unaware, they passed over you,
happy with their technological victories,
each one with their own colorful banners
bought just at the corner store.
They exchanged fake dreams:
amazing sunsets and sunrises
always ready at their fingertips,
magical cotton candy encounters,
and infinite worlds to browse.
Blood and pain
were just uncomfortable images to format.
And then the love—a last wish—
alternated like the courses of a dinner
made increasingly fast by Wi-Fi.

You stood in a dirty trench
dreaming of ancient destinations.
A daisy blossomed,
rows of real trees waited for the sunset,
the most intriguing and mysterious stories.
I was next to you in your sadness—
in this sun that did not want to be born,
holding your hand with a whisper,
"I believe in you."

If Sometimes

If sometimes you don't remember my name
and your memory wavers in search of me,
don't remove the transparent thread
that binds us like two flying kites.

If sometimes you can't see me,
even in the small mountain lake
or on our long, lonely path,
look for me in your heart.

If sometimes the wind forces us to be far away,
don't grope to reverse your flight.
Just have a little patience;
I will soon be back in front of you.

If sometimes the night seems eternal
and its shadow spreads into your soul,
close your eyes and think of me, my love!
The doors of your heart will open.

If sometimes I cry, they are not tears of sadness;
it's the thought of you that turns me.
The heart does not resist such a great emotion
and makes tears flourish like flowers in spring.

The Match

I remember a picture:
your strange smile
is stumbling
on your dolomite teeth.

So, I say,
when spring is coming,
"Thoughts are not lost
if you don't cast them away."

It was not because of the silence
or sad thoughts.
Maybe someone who had promised you help
didn't bring you where you wanted.

In the time of a match lighting
that has filled with light,
I saw the smile
of your dolomite teeth.

Domenico Corna

7. Are Strange Thoughts That

Among timeless memories, our fears present themselves, requiring their own space within us. We seem to be in the arms of an authoritarian mother while she browses them one by one so we know, accept, and love them. Even others' sadness, in a strange contagion, asks us to be part of us.

Fear

I welcome you,
coming from dust and mud,
who knocks at my door
with your load of anguish.

You come inside me arrogantly,
emptying everything.
You sit down and talk to me
about things I believed were forgotten.

You force me into your arms
as a domineering mother,
acknowledging my pain,
turning it into madness.

Now you play with my helplessness;
my fears run free.
When you go away,
nothing will be left of me.

Song for Laura

Your voice is the face of the moon—
a window of light
suddenly opened
on your stray dog's life.

Laura, distant heart,
lost in memory,
you are a sweet ambiguity of life,
a swallow carrying the autumn.

Laura, soaked by rain,
a sweet tramway's caress
turns your voice into a flower
hidden in the garden of memories.

"I live in this tired city," you said,
"Where life has no sense,
where the roads are damned empty,
and not one of the doors opens."

Laura, sweet face of the moon,
a lost memory never lived,
a man is lost in the snow
in a lonely, useless search of you.

King's Cross Station

You enter as if no one had,
as the day when it is defeated,
attacked by the darkness.

You are a premonition,
an indication of the future—
the destiny that will assault us.

The light passes through you
in a strange sensation—
the impression of not existing.

Maybe you really don't exist
if everybody's looks slip away
to the advertising on the walls.

The doors open at King's Cross Station,
and you slide out like a moment
who refuses to attach to memory.

Remains stuck to the front glass,
your hard and angry look
that takes me to the next gallery:

an illusion belongs to us,
an uncertain grip.
Everything else we have stolen.

Dance of a Raindrop

On this sad evening,
on the glass of my window,
a raindrop falls,
dancing slowly
to oblivion
like a movie star
grabbing her moment.

Between bends and imperfections,
she consumes her short life,
just imagining
the great world beyond the glass,
while my eyes
and my heart are wincing
for her every small space conquered.

Then she comes to the end of her run,
to be confused with any other,
waiting for a new sun
to take her back over there again,
dreaming of another small dance—
close to my eyes,
close to my heart.

In this endless dance,
how I wish, for a moment,
she would open her eyes
to see my smile,
to see my heart.
I would finally fall asleep
with no more pain.

From the Top of My House

From the top of my house—
over a building much higher than the sun
but as dark as much as the night,
among the shades of the morning—
I am looking for a sign of your presence
in a still-sleepy bike,
in an old lady with her load of bread and milk,
in two men in ties who bet on the world's destiny,
in a bar at the corner always offering its bitter fruits:
only a few bucks to overcome loneliness.

The sound of a distant bell
tells me you're not there but inside me,
and it brings a smile to my heart.

"Tomorrow the bicycle will raise its handlebars like
the nose of a plane and will reach the highest clouds.
The old lady will dance all day long into the sun in her
new colorful dress.
Jackets and ties will be resting on the bench, and two
men dressed in undershirts will play marbles in the
sand.
The bar on the corner will emit colored notes,
dispersing in the wind."

While I go downstairs,
meeting my day,
I think of you—of the future that will be.
So, I'm happy even if the newspaper
reports only sad news.

Spirit Mesa

Yours is the image of freedom,
your sunset,
where earth turns pink,
joining the sky,
where the clouds
ride the prairie.

Standing here, I don't know who I am—
perhaps the dust of your desert,
waiting for its wind,
perhaps a fallen dream
like those of your horses
can't fly anymore.

Standing here, I don't know who I am—
perhaps the last of your horses,
still looking for his wings.
I fear this feeling,
your past that can drag me away
and my secret dreams
on my way home.

Here is the center of the Earth;
here is the center of the Heart.
Here is love, true love,
for what was before
and will be after. Earth—
we don't own it;
we are just guests.

Hands and the Moon

When the sun goes down
and the light, as a soft reflection,
runs downhill
to the horizon,
I see among its nuances
a path through the hills
where trees and branches
come together with the sky,
where young swallows
take their first flights,
and the moon is so brave
to rest in the palm
of my hands
like a crystal ball.

She talks of the past and future,
memories and hopes
that no longer belong
to suffering or regret
but only to nostalgia,
to a tender caress
that blurs the horizon
as the light becomes night—
but slowly, without haste,
so that my thoughts
can run away,
finally free,
on an immense prairie.

Montisola's High Road

The uniform expanse of light on the other shore
forced me to the side of the road,
oblivious to the moon's warnings.
She, like every night, was about to bring to life,
the thousand sighs of the inhabitants of the forest.

I was surprised by the strange game
of the gaseous masses that, holding hands,
climbed from the lake,
making alive with flashing lights
the crib on the other side of the lake.

With one foot on the ground,
I searched among those lights for the same cloud—
the one next to my destiny—
the sweetest, the most complicated—
the one that challenged my mature age.

Then the grocery bags called me;
they were tired of hanging on the handlebars
and asked me to resume my trip
on Montisola's high road
and leave there my thousand heartbeats.

Only the smallest of my dreams
remained sighing at the edge of the forest,
among all my friends—always inside there—
always laughing at my futile search.
"It's not yet time to go back home."

Hundreds of Lights

Hundreds of lights sway gently
in their wake by bowing
the flame of the candles.
They enter the thoughts,
meeting time,
who discreetly withdraws.

They are not voices or gasps,
only a faint scent and the distance
between my eyes and your eyes.
I can draw them with my fingers,
from the contour of your lashes,
to the movement of your eyelids,
to your lips that will bend slowly
as the moon in the first quarter.

Will open up the words never said,
and nothing else is more important.

Then the hands join—
an intense moment—
the time of the leaves,
which, breaking away from the trees,
migrate to the autumn.

Behind them remains a smile—
an intangible sadness—
and that perfume
cannot be forgotten.

8. Lead Us

Our weakness makes us fall; it makes us feel like the last person in the world—abandoned and marginalized. But let us not lose heart. After every storm, the sun always returns, as the moment to rise again. When we do, it is another step toward our destination. The strength of accepting the humiliation, tears, and neglect will take us home.

A Choice

Step by step,
bent over ourselves,
with a backpack
full of desires
but getting heavier
every passing moment,

we dream of a different choice
after discovering the other side of us.
We build without limit
and come back as if we had never started.

Last Chance

Ice sparkles on your face—
the hand follows the last drop,
lost in the humidity of the rain.

Life is enclosed in that box,
accompanied by a long line of pain.

Two leaves, before falling from a tree,
together floated in the wind.
But it was yesterday—a long time ago.

I felt your eyes closed
by fear and in the difference
of who stops and who goes forward.

Your pain was like an arrow—
I looked at you, and it pierced me.

Spring changes into fall—
every time opportunities are missed,
every time the eyes don't open.

But autumn changes into spring—
the leaves come back on the trees
in the last chance.

A Real Pain

When I walk by that road,
you are in my mind's eye.
I see the life that goes away.

How may I feel hypocritical?
What is the pain value of a calf crying
in the arms of death?

I would like to chase away the responsibility
of feeding on your body—
this feeling of shame.

Instead, I offend twice a real pain
even feeding your tears.
Life went out here today.

This Path of Pain

How many tears,
how many cries hidden behind a smile?
Love and anger hold hands.

I was close to running away,
to forget forever
this path of pain—
too much like hell.

Then I met you;
your smile was that of a child.
You gave me a single moment,
one blow near my heart.
You took my fears away,
and I resumed walking
like ancient time's pilgrim
on a path of great dreams.

Now I'm strong and immense—
a thousand pains without falling.

But on this evening of poor intentions,
with moon and stars hidden,
how I wish you were here,
just touching my eyes,
and I imagine for a moment
I feel at home with you.

Like You

When I look at this world,
I am just like you—
timid, fearful, and insecure.
Like you, I lead a life I didn't want,
surrounded by anxiety.
Like you, I walk unhappily on dusty roads,
losing my good intentions every time—
barely dodging the anger.

How can we defend ourselves from hatred,
from this continuous trampling on us?

Like you, I don't put up my soul for sale.
I take the little that life gives:
a sunset, a strange flower on the path,
a fairy tale, a weird little poem,
to fall asleep, hoping to fly,
to wake up regretting the big night,
but always on the path—
two endless lines, slightly acute angle,
that at the end will meet.

Stupid Pain

If I could beat
this stupid pain,
I certainly would think of you,
of dreams, imagination,
even of bad omens
disguised as good ones.
I would not be on the sidelines
with a hand resting
on my left cheek
and my head filled
with useless thoughts
and strategies
to appease the pain
of a stupid tooth
that is forcing me
to close my poem here, now!

If the Sun Is Only Light

Today, Sun's soul does not want to rise,
standing alone beyond the sea line,
spying on a world that no longer belongs to him.
It was only yesterday that prayers implored him
and lovers played with his light,
exchanging a thousand promises.

"If light is only light, I will leave it to you.
I will go away with my loneliness,
bringing back all my children's souls:
the wind, the clouds, the children's smiles,
and the old boat of the last sailor—
his face carved by my thousand kisses and offenses."

Today, here in the city, we are left alone
to look at what remains of the Sun—
magically hidden by the smile of the Moon,
until it comes even for us—
the time to mirror our hearts
and start to dream, dream, dream…

The Lake

Like the night, like the darkness,
like a shadow who courts the moon,
with her rays, she caresses my eyes
with an unexpected wind
because I don't get lost
like a lonely dog
at the edge of the darkness,
looking for a reason.

I find your light
in the midst of a thousand shades.
Seeing her, maybe reaching
to touch her
over there, on the way home,
where the darkness does not surprise me anymore,
and the light of the fantasy
finally opens my eyes.

Two Lives

Something special
can happen to you
when you are sad
and understand the meaning
of what is not eternal.

It would be madness
to offer a different thought
to your loneliness.
It will open its veil
to a new light.

Take my hand
in a new round of dance,
in this new life
with a different fate
free from anguish.

The last hope
comes from the night
even if the day after,
a little ashamed,
you refuse to believe.

I am hidden there
among thoughts,
seemingly useless.
They lead you
close to me.

9. We Keep One Dream Alive

Time flows on this path that seems endless, while we preserve our dream by living apparently infertile seasons, hoping as soon this painful path soon end. Time, vain expectations, lost messages and normalcy are sensations that measure our strength in keeping our dreams alive.

One Day, That Day Will Come

The breath that runs through my soul
has brought a message
from an unknown sender
hidden in a distant storm now dissolved.
That little, courageous white cloud,
carried it because it could come here,

"One day, that day will come,
when darkness becomes light,
revealing its magical reasons.
Then you will raise your sails
for a journey without limits.
Oceans, continents, planets, and galaxies
will be like marbles in the sand.
You still will not know who you are,
and sinister omens will agitate your heart,
but you'll be as free as a good intention,
and you'll wake up, opening your eyes."

Your Return

When the day comes
of your return,
and the trees bow down their branches
to the new spring wind,
the scent of the cold musk
that led you away
will be just a memory.

Then I will rise,
remembering to the moon her promise
to send away
all the thoughts from your mind,
and for the first time
my face will appear to you,
this time away from your dreams.

I Stopped the Time

I stopped the tyrant time
because the Sun doesn't want to play with the Moon,
and the sad Wind is sitting here on the Wood of
Plane.
Together we talk of sadness and loneliness,
of you who were here
just a moment ago.

Together we look at that side of the path
from where you always came back;
we can't help but dream about you with us
because you are like the wind
that runs before the spring
and melts the freezing of the soul.

The Sun and Wind made me a promise;
they keep me company
to tame my sorrow
until you are here
and I hear your smile.
Only then will they return to play somewhere else.

I know you'll be all for them the next day,
but no one will have to spy on our joy
when at last we are one.

Inside the Park in My Town

Walking slowly at night,
inside the park in my town,
where ponds seem to have unfathomable depths,
where paths will soon be covered
by so many people with music in their headphones,
like roads toward the next world.
I don't want to wake up.
I don't want to come back to life.
Each time the sun calls,
I would like to stay forever
in that warm harmony
on the threshold of a soft madness.
No one told me
my path would lead to madness—
to overturn common sense—
to make probable what I feel in my heart.
How strange to have to hide my thoughts
and try to look like many others.
I sit next to the night—
sister of my soul,
the only one with whom I can talk
without fear of being discovered.

Talking to myself,
talking to you and infinity…

I walk in the park, enveloped by the dark—
the impression of victory over the common destiny.
I look forward to the first little ray of sunshine
when I wake up and go out of my house,
like many others running in the park.

The Bet

I gazed at you secretly
to your wonder,
surprising.

You stole my words
so closely,
so fast.

You gathered my thoughts
into an emotion,
amazing.

You made a bet with me,
and I have lost,
hopelessly.

Where is my strength?
Dissolved far away,
inside your smile.

True Heart

A true heart
and a clear soul
know the time
of the swallows in the spring,
the pure dream
able to modify the memories,
the pain in promise—
the sweetest place
to come back.

A true heart
and a clear soul
know how to wait for
the right moment
when emotions change—
hate and guilt
change into pain,
and melancholy finds a home
in the desire for love.

A true heart
and a clear soul
not only raise daisies
from the depths of the earth
when the time comes,
but also run anywhere,
releasing its perfume
upwind in time.

Soldiers

How many have to suffer?
If you can count.
Perhaps it was the fear
or the audacity.
But who was the winner
and who was the loser?

I felt fear
thinking of you.
I saw the terror
in cruel remorse
of what you have done
and what you could not.

Soldiers win!
Soldiers die!
But if history speaks of you,
narrating the deeds,
it does not say that the lucky ones
are those who don't come back.

Harvest

Behind the wall of the house,
the heat, the thoughts,
the songs of cicadas
in the fields of grain
next to the harvest.

Voices approach
from the folds of the day,
creeping between the branches,
between the leaves' hands,
their trembling breath.

When the farm carts approach,
the fields are ready
for a ritual need
that was their fathers,
cut out to survive.

In the evening, the screeching stops,
and the wind blows free
on land now bald.
His singing becomes sad;
nothing bows down to its flowing.

The Fog

I'm walking into the fog,
where nature itself is confused,
showing the real soul
of this soulless city.

The other half of me ran away
on a bright day.
I hug this feeling—
wet and fertile like a dream.

The sound of a distant radio
shapes the contours of melancholy.
I'm captured by the frosted light
of a shy and indulgent motor.

Somebody passes by me—
maybe he is coming home,
fluttering like a leaf,
just a moment before I confuse him.

On this November evening,
only the ghosts are happy,
immersed in the charm of sadness
and in the pleasure of feeling at home.

99

10. Hand in Hand

We are songs flying in the sky—so many souls, hand in hand, waiting at the station, each with their own weight, their long, lonely nights looking for a reason. Many identical and different paths meet themselves, and, at every junction of souls, a heat wave surprises us.

Songs Flying in the Sky

Songs fly in the sky
like swallows in the spring
looking for their nest,
those of the last season.
They carry hopeful eyes—
indefinable souls
looking like distant stars
that exist in dreams
and ancient fairy tales
when the soul becomes pure.

Songs fly in the sky
enveloped by ancient twilight,
by notes barely adverted
like the soft sighs
of two hidden lovers
who bring their souls
and exchange their hearts
in eternal promises,
in breaths
until the sun returns.

At the Station

The cold, dark, and damp of the morning
and this sun that never seems to rise—
we are all at the station waiting for the train,
holding our little warmth and little last blood
with faces down like who is always waiting for
judgment.
Maybe someone, leaning against a corner, crying
slowly,
maybe someone approaches him, brushing a little on
his heart—
he soothes his sadness to forget his own.

Toward the fog, hundreds of glances, between illusion
and anger, tightening strong, holding hand in hand.

But the train is oblivious to what was before—
sadness, darkness, and tiredness;
it knows only the warmth and the soft rhythm
of the people who open their eyes and recognize—
the life rushing fast from the window
without compromising the strength of their souls.
It just goes straight to the destination like a fairy tale.

Invisible Lover

I was quietly lying,
watching the moon coming down
from the edge of my window,
while, as happens every night, its light
is offered thousands of voices
to play with my thoughts.

But from thousands, one unknown caress
comes forward, surprising me.
He says tonight will not follow the moonlight.
He stands here next to me like a spiteful bug—
between the notes of this song,
the pages of this book,
and the voices of the people down on the street.

He whispers to me, "I want to be with you."
He blows on my hands
and ruffles my hair.
This night he sleeps with me—
will startle my heart
down to the depths of my dreams
with his warm wind of caresses.

In my lonely bed,
today has come a true lover.
I can peacefully close my eyes
because he will protect me from the sad thoughts.
The moon smiles with its last rays
and leaves my world,
slipping behind the chimney on the roof.

Teddy Bear

Just a moment ago
on the edge of infinity,
my teddy bear and I
did somersaults.
On that bright night,
he had mercy on me,
joining our hands
between the sky, moon, and stars,
up to this morning,
to the usual sad tramway
with its wet caress
and the half smile of the people.

I let myself be swallowed
by a world without fantasies,
like a tin soldier
with his cork rifle.
I translate incomprehensible sentences.
I study stupid attitudes
waiting for the coffee break
to look skyward.

A true smile surprised me today
while I was looking at a climbing squirrel
between the branches, sleepily stretching
in the rite of spring.
It gave me a message:
my teddy bear
feels so much nostalgia
for my poor heart.

Old Black-and-White Movie

How strange to see you looking at me
in this old black-and-white movie—
an old glory smiling happily
inside images running slowly
but faster than my life,
and the story that has appropriated
of my emotions and my light.

As you look at me, I am shivering.
It would be enough, only a sign from you,
and I would be ready to surrender,
to emerge from that movie,
to hold you tight in my arms,
to look into those eyes
so long dreamed of.

I would give you all my dreams
in return for one of your smiles.
I would tell you about my life,
about the useless search for you
in the eyes of all those I met
without knowing that, intentionally,
we were dispersed over time.

If you had been here with me,
no one would have dreamed with my dreams,
no one would drink from my heart,
no one but you.
So, we are two breaths lost in time
who can never meet
if not in our dreams.

Loves Chasing Each Other

Nobody is like you—
defenseless and fragile,
always about to give up,
determined to try
the simplest solution
when the situation becomes difficult.

When I look at you,
I feel nostalgia
for when I was like you
on this long and difficult path,
cursing every step,
hating myself for saying yes.

Now that calm and harmony
fill my soul,
I look at you so tenderly,
dreaming of the moment
you finally open your eyes
and everything seems like a funny dream.

One day you'll grow up—
it will be you who teaches me.
You will smile at my mistakes
in this strange, indefinable
alternation of the seasons,
of loves chasing each other.

Looking Through the Shop Windows

In front of the shop
at the street corner,
I watch at its window with greediness.
This morning I was surprised
by the desire to transform myself:
a hat, a dress,
a new belt
that would enhance my figure
and calm my sadness.

In this race against time,
I let myself be captured
by one of the thousand useless games
to change my image
while my soul is oppressed
by an infinite sadness
and my eyes are dripping
slow, silent tears,
even if I smile.

At the door of the shop,
with my package of illusions,
I face another day,
waiting for the next night
when my arms open again.
I hope whoever meets them
does not make me too bad
and, if only for a moment,
makes me forget the loneliness.

New Friendship

A dog,
with his oriental muzzle,
met my gaze
at a street corner,
squatting on the ground.
He was waiting for the end
of a very bad game—
a friendly sign
to come back.

A dog
every morning,
waiting for me under my balcony,
bites me with happiness;
for the whole day,
he follows me with his thought,
dreaming of my return,
requiring on his oriental muzzle
a good night caress.

To My Unknown Brother

How I wish you had the memory of yourself
to understand how you were before.
How much you enjoyed flying,
stealing all the colors of the rainbow.

You became as blue as your sky,
as green as your eyes,
as pink as your destiny,
and as red as the sunset.

But the most beautiful color you had inside
was my sincere love,
as white as the warmest sunshine
that leads you now on your path.

One day, my dear little brother,
you'll be lost in the sky, lonely as a cloud.
But don't worry; I'll be there waiting for you,
for you to land right here in my arms.

11. While Our Souls Overlap

One special soul is walking with us—within us. With an incomprehensible presence and unbridgeable distance, he or she makes us fall in love and measures the strength of our love. He or she loves our sighs and our conflicts in the sad days as in those shining.

White Flower

A white flower
now is playing with me
who, from the thorns,
has glimpsed the blue.

I feel the fear
of this strange darkness
and so much emptiness
inside me.

Sweet solitude—
friend and sister,
you made me glad
of your sweet taste.

I recognize you
inside the wind
and the dark moon,
who will not come out.

I leave my memory here
for everybody else,
like a small light-blue cloud
lost in the blue.

All for You

Tender with you
as never I have been,
I'll caress your wishes—
pure and true love,
for every minute of the day,
even those that don't exist,
for every fairy tale never told,
for each heart of a lover,
in every poem, every song,
only and always together.

I will trample you
harder than I have ever done.
I'll tear away your dreams one by one—
pure and true hatred,
for every minute of the day,
also beyond time.
I build the worst nightmares.
I will be your worst enemy.
You'll hate me with every curse
without being able to get me.

When finally you know who you are
and shine like the sun,
you will also discover my pain
for every breath, for each offense—
how weak was my strength,
how I have wept in solitude,
hating myself like nobody ever has,
to see you here finally—all for you.

Small Bright Pearl

An old figure goes down slowly,
bent on his shell of sadness.
His eyes can't see
the upcoming radiant dawn.

His thoughts have fought
against bloody and invisible enemies,
sowing, in his path of tears,
one seed for each time he fell.

I look at him, fascinated by his pain,
by those rare and precious tears.
I could not resist touching his eyes,
stealing away one of his tears.

That small bright pearl
has found a place in my house.
It illuminates with reflected light
ancient paintings and memories.

He left without seeing me
sliding slowly along the wall—
among thousands of eyes behind and above him
waiting for the future.

A thousand children, unknown to him,
make dance in a circle, holding hands,
and, in a long trail, scream with joy,
raising their hands to the sky.

Small Tired Pearl

What I have had
and could not give,
with a handful of useless memories,
keeps me company on this cold morning.

After having danced for a long time
between the sky, moon, and stars,
you have taken away
even the fruit of my eyes

and left me to look up,
groping in a long wait
like a tired and needless seed
not able to germinate.

It's useless for you to insist
on driving my nights;
my legs are too tired
to dance alone.

Too many times I fell;
too many times I got up.
Really, do you think I'm still happy
with this stupid and lonely dance?

Who knows why I feel your smile?
Your head is nodding and whispers,
"It's always been that way.
It has always been like that."

On the Right Side of the Road

I saw you
next to the highway,
bent over your car
unable to start.
You looked at the engine.
You looked at the sky.
I felt your thoughts,
so tired and angry
in finding yourself in the wrong place.
I wanted to go beyond.
It was enough, only a single gesture
to restart your path,
to see your smile again.
Instead, I'm always here
on the right side of the road
to contemplate your anger
and the thin rain of tears
descending slowly.
You'll see. The rain will stop,
and you will find the failure
and the reason to resume your run.
I, as always,
will be here on the right side of the road.

On the Left Side of the Road

My car stopped
on the left side of the road
during this long, empty run—
sad, boring, and indefinable
that never seems to end.

But where is your comfort?
"You'll never be alone," you said,
"On the left side of the road."
Instead, I'm leaning here
without the desire to start again.

I know you are hidden, sitting somewhere
on the right side of the road
while you calculate my sadness,
waiting for a nod
that makes you indispensable.

But I don't ask for compassion.
I will not cry for help.
I will make this stupid car start again.
I will raise my eyes as before,
on that long path, to go.

Little Cheat

Enveloped by loneliness,
I sit down on the bench,
watching the swallows fly—
the hands and the wings of the children.

I searched long for the thought of you
between the rays of the setting sun,
but today only sadness
has been added to my loneliness.

So, I wait for the coming night,
sitting between my saddest thoughts,
which evoke all the tears of the world
to help my intention.

I will not move from the bench.
I will not be cured by the people passing by
with their smiles of compassion
that offend more than insults.

I'll wait for the moon to rise,
with my soul immersed in the darkest darkness,
to push my pain beyond the rational,
simulating hopeless despair.

You'll sit next to me
to give me a smile and your caresses.
I hope you don't notice my little trick
to get a little love.

The River from Your Window

The river comes to your window,
looking inside to discover if you kept your promise
to present you both at the appointed time.
He would like to know if you have loved each other.
Before he drags you on, with the power he is allowed,
he will look into your two souls,
erasing every memory and canceling,
one by one, your every obligation.

For a moment you will experience real solitude—
no longer the union to form a soul,
but many lonely points of light
scattered in the dark in fervent research.
In that poetic current's game,
a thousand other lights will approach you
with the intention of loving you—
to build together a new soul for a new life.

Maybe you two will create one soul,
starting a new adventure
in love and hate's game of life
waiting for the river to bring you back here again.
Maybe you will never know
I am one of those small, bright, lonely spots
far away from the impetuous flow—
here, forever waiting for you.

I could not forget
that once I was part of you.
I can't promise to love anyone else
because it would be a lie.

Before the Sea Line

When the sea line bends the horizon
in a wide embrace,
when you miss the meaning of life,
the alternation of time as waves
scratching even the most resistant rocks;
when you think that the time has come
to make sense of your sunset,
among so many tears and some nostalgia,
between smiles too far away
and a life that crumbles as slowly
as thin, annoying sand…

Hug me before life surprises us
and makes fun of us another time.
Let us fall in love because memory sustains us.
We are two grains of colored sand
waiting to be lifted by the wind
in two children's games.
Two lives will turn happily in the vortex—
in the arms of the wind toward the horizon,
where the sun kisses the sea line
and soothes the sadness of two tired little souls,
never more unhappy—finally pure.

121

12. Until the End of the Path

We find that, in the game of time, our path is finished before it begins. Our eyes open to a new beginning while the dark becomes just a game to remember how it was before. We are free, and the fantasy, at last understandable, shows us the direction toward our true home. Nothing is more amazing than when love fulfills our wishes.

So, It Happens

So, it happens
when fear rises,
when nobody calls you,
feeling lost, victim of yourself,
without any chance of getting out.

Perhaps a shell
you have put inside,
freeing your prisoners,
cutting by yourself at every chance
you vile, sad, outcasts, last in this world.

Raise your hands.
This is your moment,
the time of your hard battle.
You can't be defeated if you don't want it.
Don't hide yourself with unnecessary defenses.

Live in the moment.
Your next magical destiny
is taking place in front of you.
Take your weaknesses by the hand,
sad commander of countless defeats.

Here, victory
is finally fulfilled.
Widen your tired arms,
welcome the wind to your heart,
and finally accept the long-sought happiness.

Remember

Our thousand dialogues
were not built to gain applause,
to warm your heart in sad moments.
I entered your heart.

Hold me tight because I am a precious gift.
I will not support you on your long path.
I will not help you to calm the nightmares.
I will not be a secure grip
or the thought that becomes truth.

I will help you with what is most precious:
getting a clear soul.
Your light will never go out,
your heart will be harder than misfortunes
and softer than anxieties.

You'll never win your war,
but eventually time will tire of fighting
a bowling pin that continually rises,
and then he will forget you.

You will be a small anomaly
in a world that is not yours,
that will never adapt to you.
Your spirit will be located elsewhere,
finally free to go back home.

All Right

It's all right if you wake up at night and think of me
without being able to fall asleep,
if, when you walk down the road,
you look for me in the eyes of the people you meet,
hoping for a revelation.

It's all right if, at night, the pain holds you,
keeping you company until awakening,
if you think at any moment,
the ax is on the verge
of falling down on your head.

It's all right if your friends forsake you
like a shame to be avoided,
if, when they meet you on the street,
they turn their gazes toward advertisements
until you pass beyond.

It's fear and shame
to make them forget you
forcing you to be alone.
For you, it's the madness
of the mixed and shattered limits.

I promised you!
I'll always be on your side
in not letting you understand,
in denying you any applause
so, you don't miss your appointment.

Next Generation

When harmony wakes up your heart
and asks you to bend over once again
and put on your old shoes,
you'll see—they will adapt
to the sharp stones of this generation—
stupid and vainglorious.

When gained freedom
amazes your desires,
there are no wings on your passing
nor a flower to celebrate you.
Instead, you will know that on top of the old slavery,
another one will overlay—
bitter and poignant, even if poetic and imaginative.

So, it has always been,
from generation to generation, start after start,
with no apparent reason.
Even the sun of this generation
will not warm your heart
but will give you a thousand invisible faces
who listen to you in disbelief.

They open their hearts
only when the fear of the dark
is the reflection of their souls.
They look for you,
imploring you that your gentle caress
pacifies their pain.

Wake Up

Wake up! Open your eyes!
The sun is high
in this cloudless
spring.

The warmth dried
our long path,
and many flowers are born
in place of the swamps.

Come and get me!
The night is close,
and I'm too tired
to play with the pain.

Even if I hide myself,
keeping close the memories
like flowers in my arms,
I have no way to escape.

The wind knows how to find me;
he will steal my soul
and force me to spend an entire life
searching for you again.

Please wake up
and take my hand
as you promised—
before the night comes back.

The Gate of the Sun

Summer time has come,
shaking the scent of love.
It woke you up when you did not believe—
a spider's web had been dropped down.

It entered by the gate of the sun
and surprised your empty house
like a friend who covers your eyes with her hands,
asking you to search through your memories.

Hazy childhood nostalgia—
her voice has the color of the dreams
of a distant storm
that makes a child hide in bed.

"Your path goes downhill now—
everybody's waiting for your arrival.
They are jumping with happiness
just to see your sweet smile."

Sweet country road downhill—
it's fruitful when the rain falls
and shatters when the sun is too strong.
This is the Wood of Plane.

The Last Mile

Near the town of our wishes,
your eyes light up
at the gate of a hotel
at the beginning of the day.

You gently pause and grab the taste
of a simple, small pleasure
while, squeezing your eyes,
you let go in sweet surrender.

Sad thoughts
run so far away,
unable to scratch
the smile surrounding you.

Maybe the magic you were waiting for
had to happen later,
beyond the river or on the boulevard,
among desires and memories.

Maybe you still have not realized,
but unexpectedly, it broke free here,
and now you can be wherever you want:
here now or lost on the horizon.

On the Top of the Hill

We again took the school bag
to learn not to make ourselves into Somebody.
We left our important personalities
hidden in equations unresolved,

between books, songs, denied answers,
in the need to grab the becoming,
in a presence, a hidden love,
in a close answer not revealed.

We'll get to the top of the hill
with our love and hands free,
with missed opportunities,
wet rooms, and an ancient smell.

Barefoot, we'll knock on the door
asking permission to enter.
The wind will break the memories
and I won't be able to put them in order.

We've reached the top of the hill,
maybe we came all together.
With our eyes toward another sun,
we shall fly holding hands.

The End of the Path

When you reach
the end of the path,
where light and dark
don't exist,
where life and death
don't exist—
just emptiness and you.
You will experience real solitude.
What you have lived
will seem an illusion,
a game of your mind,
oppressed out of nowhere.
Don't be afraid:
the beginning of everything
is always emptiness.
I'll wait for you.
We will be one,
as in the beginning.
Welcome me;
we'll take each other's hands,
we'll turn around,
we'll build
a new world,
spreading the scent
of our souls
and many small traces
to everyone else's path.

9 791281 450097